D0828158

Blankets for *Toddlers*

With these 12 simple patterns, you can create 24 blankets that are "just right" for any season. See pages 2-3 to find out how.

LEISURE ARTS, INC.
Maumelle, Arkansas

INTRODUCTION

Making soft wraps for toddlers couldn't be easier!

Each of the 12 blanket designs in this book is
rated Beginner or Easy skill level and uses medium
weight yarn in a simple one-row pattern repeat.

To give you a choice of making a lighter weight blanket or a
heavier one, the instructions are all written for both a
Single Strand version and a Double Strand version.

That's 24 different blankets from this one book —
what a super value!

No matter which version you choose, your
Single Strand or Double Strand blankets will have the same
finished size — because we've done all the math for you.

Color coding in the Shopping List and Instructions helps you see
how your choice affects the amount of yarn needed, the size of
hook to use, and the number of stitches for your starting chain.

All you have to do is select a pattern, decide on
Single Strand or Double Strand, and get started!

The photos on this page compare the Single Strand and Double Strand versions of the Story Time afghan from page 22.

Although both photos represent the same size area, notice that the Single Strand version shows more pattern repeats than the Double Strand version. This is why the instructions call for more stitches in the Single Strand version. The bulk of using two strands held together makes the Double Strand version need fewer stitches to produce the same size blanket.

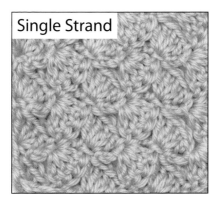

Single Strand

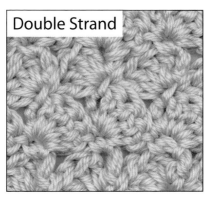

Double Strand

Nap Time

 **EASY**

SHOPPING LIST

Yarn (Medium Weight) 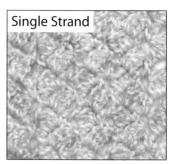 MEDIUM 4
[3.5 ounces, 190 yards
(100 grams, 173 meters) per skein]:
☐ 7{11} skeins

Crochet Hook
☐ Single Strand: Size I (5.5 mm)
☐ Double Strand: Size M/N (9 mm)
or size needed for gauge

SIZE INFORMATION
Finished Size: 36" x 45"
   (91.5 cm x 114.5 cm)

Size Note: We have printed the
instructions for Single Strand and
Double Strand versions in different
colors to make it easier for you to
find:
• Single Strand in Blue
• Double Strand (holding two strands
  of yarn together as one) in Pink
Instructions in Black apply to both
versions.

Our photography model
is a Double Strand blanket.

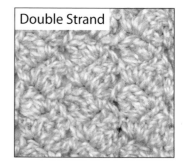

Single Strand

Double Strand

GAUGE INFORMATION

Single Strand, in pattern,
 4 repeats and 8 rows = 4" (10 cm)
Gauge Swatch: 5"w x 4"h
 (12.75 cm x 10 cm)
Ch 22.
Work same as blanket for 8 rows;
finish off: 4 Clusters.

Double Strand, in pattern,
 4 repeats and 8 rows = 6"
 (15.25 cm)
Gauge Swatch: 7¹/₂"w x 6"h
 (19 cm x 15.25 cm)
Ch 22.
Work same as blanket for 8 rows;
finish off: 4 Clusters.

─── STITCH GUIDE ───

CLUSTER (uses one st or sp)
★ YO, insert hook in st or sp
indicated, YO and pull up a loop,
YO and draw through 2 loops on
hook; repeat from ★ 2 times **more**,
YO and draw through all 4 loops
on hook.

INSTRUCTIONS

Ch 146{98}.

Row 1: Work Cluster in fifth ch
from hook, ch 1, skip next 2 chs, sc
in next ch, ★ ch 3, work Cluster in
next ch, ch 1, skip next 2 chs, sc in
next ch; repeat from ★ across to
last 2 chs, ch 2, skip next ch, dc in
last ch: 35{23} Clusters.

Row 2: Ch 4, turn; work Cluster
in first ch-2 sp, ch 1, ★ skip next
Cluster, (sc, ch 3, work Cluster)
in next ch-3 sp, ch 1; repeat
from ★ across to last ch-1 sp,
sc in last ch-1 sp, ch 2, skip last
Cluster and next ch, dc in next ch:
35{23} Clusters.

Repeat Row 2 for pattern until
blanket measures approximately
45" (114.5 cm) from beginning ch.

Finish off.

quiet moment

Shown on page 9.

 **EASY**

SHOPPING LIST

Yarn (Medium Weight)
[7 ounces, 364 yards
(198 grams, 333 meters) per skein]:
☐ 4{7} skeins

Crochet Hook
☐ **Single Strand:** Size I (5.5 mm)
☐ **Double strand:** Size M/N (9 mm)
or size needed for gauge

SIZE INFORMATION
Finished Size: 36" x 45¹/₂"
(91.5 cm x 115.5 cm)

Size Note: We have printed the
instructions for Single Strand and
Double Strand versions in different
colors to make it easier for you to
find:
• Single Strand in Blue
• Double Strand (holding two strands
of yarn together as one) in Pink
Instructions in Black apply to both
versions.

Our photography model
is a Double Strand blanket.

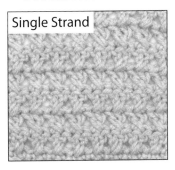
Single Strand

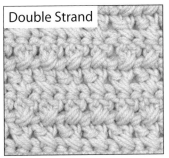
Double Strand

7

GAUGE INFORMATION

Single Strand, in pattern,
    6 Cross Sts = 4" (10 cm),
    6 rows = 4$\frac{1}{4}$" (10.75 cm)
Gauge Swatch: 4$\frac{1}{2}$" (11.5 cm)
    square
Ch 15.
Work same as blanket for 7 rows;
finish off: 6 Cross Sts and 2 dc.

Double Strand, in pattern,
    8 Cross Sts and 8 rows = 6"
    (15.25 cm)
Gauge Swatch: 6$\frac{3}{4}$"w x 6$\frac{1}{2}$"h
    (17.25 cm x 16.5 cm)
Ch 19.
Work same as blanket for 9 rows;
finish off: 8 Cross Sts and 2 dc.

INSTRUCTIONS

Each row is worked across length of blanket.

Ch 137{123}.

Row 1: Sc in second ch from hook and in each ch across: 136{122} sc.

Row 2: Ch 2 (**counts as first dc**), turn; ★ skip next st, dc in next st, 📹 working **around** dc just made (*Fig. 1, page 47*), dc in skipped st (**Cross St made**); repeat from ★ across to last st, dc in last st: 67{60} Cross Sts and 2 dc.

Repeat Row 2 for pattern until blanket measures approximately 35$\frac{3}{4}${35$\frac{1}{2}$}"/91{90} cm from beginning ch.

Last Row: Ch 1, turn; sc in each st across; finish off.

sweetie pie

SHOPPING LIST

Yarn (Medium Weight) 🄸4🄸
[3.5 ounces, 205 yards
(100 grams, 187 meters) per skein]:
☐ 7{10} skeins

Crochet Hook
☐ **Single Strand:** Size I (5.5 mm)
☐ **Double Strand:** Size M/N (9 mm)
   or size needed for gauge

SIZE INFORMATION
Finished Size: 36" x 45¹/₂"
   (91.5 cm x 115.5 cm)

Size Note: We have printed the instructions for Single Strand and Double Strand versions in different colors to make it easier for you to find:
• Single Strand in Blue
• Double Strand (holding two strands of yarn together as one) in Pink
Instructions in Black apply to both versions.

Our photography model
is a Single Strand blanket.

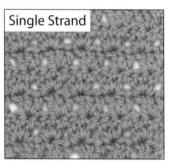

Single Strand

Double Strand

GAUGE INFORMATION

Single Strand, in pattern,
5 3-dc groups (15 sts) and 7 rows
 = 4" (10 cm)
Gauge Swatch: 4$\frac{1}{2}$"w x 4"h
 (11.5 cm x 10 cm)
Ch 19.
Work same as Body for 7 rows;
finish off: 5 3-dc groups and 2 dc.

Double Strand, in pattern,
5 3-dc groups (15 sts) and 7 rows
 = 6$\frac{1}{2}$" (16.5 cm)
Gauge Swatch: 7$\frac{1}{2}$"w x 6$\frac{1}{2}$"h
 (19 cm x 16.5 cm)
Ch 19.
Work same as Body for 7 rows;
finish off: 5 3-dc groups and 2 dc.

INSTRUCTIONS
BODY

Each row is worked across length
of blanket.

Ch 169{103}; place a marker
in third ch from hook to mark
Edging placement.

Row 1 (Wrong side)**:** 3 Dc in
fourth ch from hook (**3 skipped
chs count as first dc**), (skip next
2 chs, 3 dc in next ch) across to
last 3 chs, skip next 2 chs, dc in
last ch: 55{33} 3-dc groups and
2 dc.

Note: Loop a short piece of yarn
around the **back** of any stitch on
Row 1 to mark **right** side.

Row 2: Ch 3 (**counts as first dc**),
turn; 3 dc in next dc, (skip next
2 dc, 3 dc in next dc) across to last
3 dc, skip next 2 dc, dc in last dc.

Repeat Row 2 for pattern until
Body measures approximately
35{34$\frac{1}{2}$}"/89{87.5} cm from
beginning ch, ending by working
a **right** side row; do **not** finish off.

EDGING

Rnd 1: Ch 1, turn; 3 sc in first dc, sc in next dc and in each dc across to last dc, 3 sc in last dc; work 131{79} sc evenly spaced across end of rows;  working in free loops of beginning ch *(Fig. 2, page 47)*, 3 sc in first ch, sc in next ch and in each ch across to marked ch, 3 sc in marked ch; work 131{79} sc evenly spaced across end of rows; join with slip st to first sc: 604{368} sc.

Rnd 2: Ch 1, turn; ★ (sc in next sc, ch 3, skip next sc) across to center sc of next corner 3-sc group, (sc, ch 3) twice in center sc, skip next sc; repeat from ★ around; join with slip st to first sc, finish off.

rock-a-bye

 **EASY**

SHOPPING LIST

Yarn (Medium Weight) 🔢4
[5 ounces, 256 yards
(141 grams, 234 meters) per skein]:
☐ 5{8} skeins

Crochet Hook
☐ **Single Strand:** Size I (5.5 mm)
☐ **Double Strand:** Size M/N (9 mm)
or size needed for gauge

SIZE INFORMATION
Finished Size: 35¹/₂{36}" x 45"
  [90{91.5} cm x 114.5 cm]

Size Note: We have printed the
instructions for Single Strand and
Double Strand versions in different
colors to make it easier for you to
find:
• Single Strand in Blue
• Double Strand (holding two strands
  of yarn together as one) in Pink
Instructions in Black apply to both
versions.

Our photography model
is a Double Strand blanket.

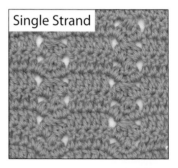
Single Strand

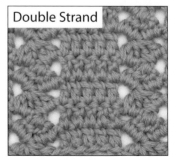
Double Strand

GAUGE INFORMATION

Single Strand, in pattern,
2 repeats = 5" (12.75 cm),
7 rows = 4½" (11.5 cm)

Gauge Swatch: 6¼"w x 4½"h
(16 cm x 11.5 cm)

Ch 27.

Work same as Body for 7 rows; finish off: 2 Clusters, 4 ch-2 sps, and 15 dc.

Double Strand, in pattern,
2 repeats = 8" (20.25 cm),
5 rows = 4" (10 cm)

Gauge Swatch: 10"w x 4"h
(25.5 cm x 10 cm)

Ch 27.

Work same as Body for 5 rows; finish off: 2 Clusters, 4 ch-2 sps, and 15 dc.

— STITCH GUIDE —

BEGINNING CLUSTER
(uses next 5 chs)

★ † YO, insert hook in **next** ch, YO and pull up a loop, YO and draw through 2 loops on hook; repeat from ★ once **more** †, skip next ch, repeat from † to † once, YO and draw through all 5 loops on hook.

CLUSTER (uses next 2 ch-2 sps)

★ YO, insert hook in **next** ch-2 sp, YO and pull up a loop, YO and draw through 2 loops on hook, YO, insert hook in **same** ch-2 sp, YO and pull up a loop, YO and draw through 2 loops on hook; repeat from ★ once **more**, YO and draw through all 5 loops on hook.

INSTRUCTIONS
BODY
Ch 137{87}.

Row 1: Dc in fourth ch from hook **(3 skipped chs count as first dc)** and in next 3 chs, ★ ch 2, work Beginning Cluster, ch 2, dc in next 5 chs; repeat from ★ across: 13{8} Clusters, 26{16} ch-2 sps, and 70{45} dc.

Row 2: Ch 3 **(counts as first dc, now and throughout)**, turn; dc in next 4 dc, ★ ch 2, work Cluster, ch 2, dc in next 5 dc; repeat from ★ across.

Repeat Row 2 for pattern until Body measures approximately 43¹/₄{43}"/110{109} cm from beginning ch; do **not** finish off.

EDGING
Rnd 1: Ch 1, turn; 2 sc in first dc, work a multiple of 3 sc evenly spaced across *(see Multiples, page 45)*, (3 sc in corner, work a multiple of 3 sc evenly spaced across) 3 times, sc in same st as first sc; join with slip st to first sc.

Rnd 2: Ch 3, turn; (2 dc, ch 1, 3 dc) in same st, skip next 2 sc, ★ † (2 dc, ch 1, 2 dc) in next sc, skip next 2 sc †; repeat from † to † across to center sc of next corner 3-sc group, (3 dc, ch 1, 3 dc) in center sc, skip next 2 sc; repeat from ★ 2 times **more**, then repeat from † to † across; join with slip st to first dc, finish off.

17

Party Time

SHOPPING LIST

Yarn (Medium Weight)
[4 ounces, 204 yards
(113 grams, 187 meters) per skein]:
☐ 7{11} skeins

Crochet Hook
☐ Single Strand: Size I (5.5 mm)
☐ Double Strand: Size M/N (9 mm)
   or size needed for gauge

SIZE INFORMATION
Finished Size: 36¹/₂{36³/₄}" x 45"
   [92.5{93.5} cm x 114.5 cm]

Size Note: We have printed the instructions for Single Strand and Double Strand versions in different colors to make it easier for you to find:
• Single Strand in Blue
• Double Strand (holding two strands of yarn together as one) in Pink
Instructions in Black apply to both versions.

Our photography model is a Single Strand blanket.

Single Strand

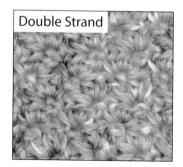
Double Strand

GAUGE INFORMATION

Single Strand, in pattern,
5 3-st groups (15 sts) and 9 rows
= 4" (10 cm)
Gauge Swatch: 4¹/₂"w x 4"h
(11.5 cm x 10 cm)
Ch 19.
Work same as Body for 9 rows;
finish off: 5 3-st groups and 1 dc.

Double Strand, in pattern,
4 3-st groups (12 sts) = 5"
(12.75 cm),
6 rows = 4" (10 cm)
Gauge Swatch: 6"w x 4"h
(15.25 cm x 10 cm)
Ch 16.
Work same as Body for 6 rows;
finish off: 4 3-st groups and 1 dc.

INSTRUCTIONS
BODY

Ch 133{85}; place a marker in third ch from hook to mark Edging placement.

Row 1 (Right side)**:** (Sc, hdc, dc) in fourth ch from hook, ★ skip next 2 chs, (sc, hdc, dc) in next ch; repeat from ★ across to last 3 chs, skip next 2 chs, dc in last ch: 43{27} 3-st groups and 1 dc.

Note: Loop a short piece of yarn around any stitch to mark Row 1 as **right** side.

Row 2: Ch 2, turn; skip first dc, (sc, hdc, dc) in next dc, ★ skip next 2 sts, (sc, hdc, dc) in next dc; repeat from ★ across to hdc of last 3-st group, skip next 2 sts, dc in top of turning ch.

Repeat Row 2 for pattern until Body measures approximately 43¹/₂{43}"/110.5{109} cm from beginning ch, ending by working a **wrong** side row; do **not** finish off.

EDGING

Rnd 1: Ch 1, turn; 3 sc in first dc, sc in each st across to turning ch, 3 sc in turning ch; work an odd number of sc evenly across end of rows;  working in free loops of beginning ch *(Fig. 2, page 47)* and in sps, 3 sc in first ch, (2 sc in next sp, sc in next ch) across to marked ch, 3 sc in marked ch; work an odd number of sc evenly across end of rows; join with slip st to first sc.

Rnd 2: Ch 1, turn; sc in each sc around, working 3 sc in center sc of each corner 3-sc group; join with slip st to first sc.

Rnd 3: Ch 4, turn; skip next sc, slip st in center sc of corner 3-sc group, ★ ch 4, skip next sc, slip st in next sc; repeat from ★ around working last slip st in slip st at base of beginning ch-4; finish off.

STORY Time

 **EASY**

SHOPPING LIST

Yarn (Medium Weight) 4
[5 ounces, 256 yards
(141 grams, 234 meters) per skein]:
☐ 7{9} skeins

Crochet Hook
☐ **Single Strand:** Size I (5.5 mm)
☐ **Double Strand:** Size M/N (9 mm)
or size needed for gauge

SIZE INFORMATION
Finished Size: 36" x 45{44¹/₂}"
[91.5 cm x 114.5{113} cm]

Size Note: We have printed the
instructions for Single Strand and
Double Strand versions in different
colors to make it easier for you to
find:
• Single Strand in Blue
• Double Strand (holding two strands
  of yarn together as one) in Pink
Instructions in Black apply to both
versions.

Our photography model
is a Single Strand blanket.

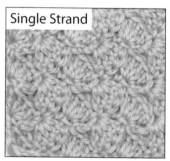
Single Strand

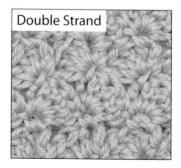
Double Strand

GAUGE INFORMATION

Single Strand, in pattern,
   4 groups = 3¹/₂" (9 cm),
   6 rows = 4" (10 cm)
Gauge Swatch: 3³/₄"w x 4"h
   (9.5 cm x 10 cm)
Ch 20.
Work same as blanket for 6 rows;
finish off: 4 groups and 1 sc.

Double Strand, in pattern,
   3 groups = 4¹/₄" (10.75 cm),
   4 rows = 4³/₄" (12 cm)
Gauge Swatch: 4³/₄" (12 cm)
   square
Ch 16.
Work same as blanket for 4 rows;
finish off: 3 groups and 1 sc.

INSTRUCTIONS

Each row is worked across length
of blanket.

Ch 208{128}.

Row 1: 4 Dc in fourth ch from
hook, ★ skip next 3 chs, (sc, ch 2,
4 dc) in next ch; repeat from ★
across to last 4 chs, skip next 3 chs,
sc in last ch: 51{31} groups and 1 sc.

Row 2: Ch 5, turn; 4 dc in fourth
ch from hook, ★ skip 4 dc of next
group, sc in ch-2 sp, ch 2, 4 dc
🎥 in side of sc just made *(Fig. A)*;
repeat from ★ across to last group,
skip 4 dc of last group, sc in ch-sp.

Fig. A

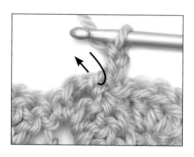

Repeat Row 2 for pattern until
blanket measures approximately
36" (91.5 cm) from beginning ch.

Last Row: Ch 5, turn; ★ skip 4 dc
of next group, sc in ch-2 sp, ch 3;
repeat from ★ across to last group,
skip 4 dc of last group, sc in ch-sp;
finish off.

SUNSHiNe

Shown on page 27.

 BEGINNER

SHOPPING LIST

Yarn (Medium Weight)
[4 ounces, 203 yards
(113 grams, 186 meters) per skein]:
☐ 8{11} skeins

Crochet Hook
☐ Single Strand: Size I (5.5 mm)
☐ Double Strand: Size M/N (9 mm)
or size needed for gauge

SIZE INFORMATION
Finished Size: 36{36¹/₂}" x 45"
[91.5{92.5} cm x 114.5 cm]

Size Note: We have printed the instructions for Single Strand and Double Strand versions in different colors to make it easier for you to find:
• Single Strand in Blue
• Double Strand (holding two strands of yarn together as one) in Pink
Instructions in Black apply to both versions.

Our photography model is a Single Strand blanket.

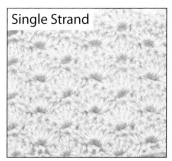
Single Strand

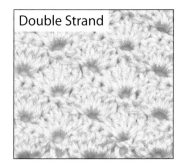
Double Strand

25

GAUGE INFORMATION

Single Strand, in pattern,
3 repeats (18 sts) = 5¹/₂" (14 cm),
6 rows = 3" (7.5 cm)
Gauge Swatch: 6³/₄"w x 3"h
(17.25 cm x 7.5 cm)
Ch 25.
Work same as blanket for 6 rows;
finish off: 4 sc and 3 5-dc groups.

Double Strand, in pattern,
3 repeats (18 sts) = 7" (17.75 cm),
6 rows = 4" (10 cm)
Gauge Swatch: 8¹/₂"w x 4"h
(21.5 cm x 10 cm)
Ch 25.
Work same as blanket for 6 rows;
finish off: 4 sc and 3 5-dc groups.

INSTRUCTIONS

Ch 121{97}.

Row 1: 2 Dc in fourth ch from hook **(3 skipped chs count as first dc)**, skip next 2 chs, sc in next ch, ★ skip next 2 chs, 5 dc in next ch, skip next 2 chs, sc in next ch; repeat from ★ across: 20{16} sc and 19{15} 5-dc groups.

Row 2: Ch 3 **(counts as first dc)**, turn; 2 dc in first sc, skip next 2 dc, sc in next dc, ★ skip next 2 dc, 5 dc in next sc, skip next 2 dc, sc in next dc; repeat from ★ across.

Repeat Row 2 for pattern until blanket measures approximately 45" (114.5 cm) from beginning ch.

Finish off.

CLOUD SOFT

SHOPPING LIST

Yarn (Medium Weight) 🧶 **4**
[5 ounces, 256 yards
(141 grams, 234 meters) per skein]:
☐ 7{11} skeins

Crochet Hook
☐ **Single Strand:** Size I (5.5 mm)
☐ **Double Strand:** Size M/N (9 mm)
  or size needed for gauge

SIZE INFORMATION

Finished Size: 36¼" x 45"
  (92 cm x 114.5 cm)

Size Note: We have printed the instructions for Single Strand and Double Strand versions in different colors to make it easier for you to find:
• Single Strand in Blue
• Double Strand (holding two strands of yarn together as one) in Pink
Instructions in Black apply to both versions.

Our photography model
is a Double Strand blanket.

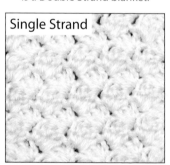
Single Strand

Double Strand

GAUGE INFORMATION

Single Strand, in pattern,
  5 3-st groups (15 sts) = 4" (10 cm),
  10 rows = 4¹/₄" (10.75 cm)
Gauge Swatch: 4¹/₄" (10.75 cm)
  square
Ch 17.
Work same as blanket for 10 rows;
finish off: 5 3-st groups and 1 sc.

Double Strand, in pattern,
  3 3-st groups (9 sts) and 6 rows =
  3¹/₄" (8.25 cm)
Gauge Swatch: 3³/₄"w x 3¹/₄"h
  (9.5 cm x 8.25 cm)
Ch 11.
Work same as blanket for 6 rows;
finish off: 3 3-st groups and 1 sc.

INSTRUCTIONS

Ch 137{101}.

Row 1: (Sc, 2 dc) in second ch from
hook, ★ skip next 2 chs, (sc, 2 dc)
in next ch; repeat from ★ across to
last 3 chs, skip next 2 chs, sc in last
ch: 45{33} 3-st groups and 1 sc.

Row 2: Ch 1, turn; (sc, 2 dc) in first
sc, ★ skip next 2 dc, (sc, 2 dc) in
next sc; repeat from ★ across to last
3 sts, skip next 2 dc, sc in last sc.

Repeat Row 2 for pattern until
blanket measures approximately
45" (114.5 cm) from beginning ch;
finish off.

CUDDLER

Shown on page 33.

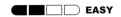 **EASY**

SHOPPING LIST

Yarn (Medium Weight) 🔵 **4**
[16 ounces, 1,020 yards
(454 grams, 932 meters) per skein]:
☐ 2 skeins

Crochet Hook
☐ **Single Strand:** Size I (5.5 mm)
☐ **Double Strand:** Size M/N (9 mm)
or size needed for gauge

SIZE INFORMATION
Finished Size: 34³/₄{36}" x 45"
[88.5{91.5} cm x 114.5 cm]

Size Note: We have printed the instructions for Single Strand and Double Strand versions in different colors to make it easier for you to find:
• Single Strand in Blue
• Double Strand (holding two strands of yarn together as one) in Pink
Instructions in Black apply to both versions.

Our photography model
is a Double Strand blanket.

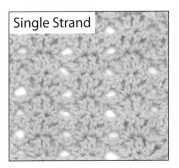

Single Strand

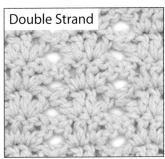

Double Strand

31

GAUGE INFORMATION

Single Strand, in pattern,
  4 repeats (16 dc) and 8 rows =
  4³/₄" (12 cm)
Gauge Swatch: 4³/₄" (12 cm)
  square
Ch 28.
Work same as Body for 8 rows;
finish off: 8 ch-1 sps and 16 dc.

Double Strand, in pattern,
  4 repeats (16 dc) = 8" (20.25 cm),
  5 rows = 4" (10 cm)
Gauge Swatch: 8"w x 4"h
  (20.25 cm x 10 cm)
Ch 28.
Work same as Body for 5 rows;
finish off: 8 ch-1 sps and 16 dc.

INSTRUCTIONS
BODY
Ch 172{106}.

Row 1: Dc in fifth ch from hook
**(4 skipped chs count as first dc
plus ch 1),** ★ skip next 4 chs, (dc,
ch 1, dc) in each of next 2 chs;
repeat from ★ across to last 5 chs,
skip next 4 chs, (dc, ch 1, dc) in last
ch: 56{34} ch-1 sps and 112{68} dc.

Row 2: Ch 4 **(counts as first dc plus
ch 1),** turn; dc in first dc, ★ skip
next 2 ch-1 sps, (dc, ch 1, dc) in
each of next 2 dc; repeat from ★
across to last 2 ch-1 sps, skip last
2 ch-1 sps, (dc, ch 1, dc) in last dc.

Repeat Row 2 for pattern until
Body measures approximately
43¹/₂{43}"/110.5{109} cm from
beginning ch; do **not** finish off.

EDGING
Rnd 1: Ch 1, turn; 3 sc in first
dc, work a multiple of 3 sc *(see
Multiples, page 45)* evenly spaced
across each side *(Fig. 2, page 47)*,
working 3 sc in each corner; join
with slip st to first sc.

Rnd 2: Ch 1, do **not** turn;
★ (sc, ch 3, 2 dc) in next sc, skip
next 2 sc; repeat from ★ around;
join with slip st to first sc, finish off.

FUN Time

SHOPPING LIST

Yarn (Medium Weight)  4
[6 ounces, 315 yards
(170 grams, 288 meters) per skein]:
☐ 5{7} skeins

Crochet Hook
☐ **Single Strand:** Size I (5.5 mm)
☐ **Double Strand:** Size M/N (9 mm)
or size needed for gauge

SIZE INFORMATION
Finished Size: 37" x 45"
  (94 cm x 114.5 cm)

Size Note: We have printed the instructions for Single Strand and Double Strand versions in different colors to make it easier for you to find:
• Single Strand in Blue
• Double Strand (holding two strands of yarn together as one) in Pink
Instructions in Black apply to both versions.

Our photography model is a Double Strand blanket.

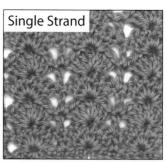

Single Strand

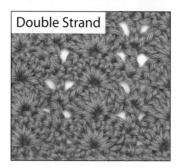

Double Strand

GAUGE INFORMATION

Single Strand, in pattern,
2 repeats (16 sts) and 5 rows =
3¹/₄" (8.25 cm)
Gauge Swatch: 3¹/₂" (9 cm) square
Ch 14.
Work same as Body for 6 rows;
finish off: 2 7-dc groups and 3 dc.

Double Strand, in pattern,
2 repeats (16 sts) and 5 rows =
5" (12.75 cm)
Gauge Swatch: 5¹/₂" (14 cm)
square
Ch 14.
Work same as Body for 6 rows;
finish off: 2 7-dc groups and 3 dc.

INSTRUCTIONS
BODY

Ch 134{86}.

Row 1 (Right side)**:** Sc in second ch
from hook and in each ch across:
133{85} sc.

Note: Loop a short piece of yarn
around any stitch to mark Row 1 as
right side.

Row 2: Ch 3 **(counts as first dc,
now and throughout)**, turn; ★ skip
next 2 sc, 7 dc in next sc, skip next
2 sc, dc in next sc; repeat from ★
across: 22{14} 7-dc groups and
23{15} dc.

Row 3: Ch 3, turn; ★ skip next 3 dc,
7 dc in next dc, skip next 3 dc, dc in
next dc; repeat from ★ across.

Repeat Row 3 for pattern until
Body measures approximately
44¹/₄{43³/₄}"/112.5{111} cm from
beginning ch, ending by working a
right side row; do **not** finish off.

EDGING

Ch 1, do **not** turn; working around dc at end of rows, (sc, ch 3, sc) in first row, 5 dc in next row, (sc in next row, 5 dc in next row) across to last sc row, skip last sc row; (sc, ch 3, sc) in  free loop of ch at base of first sc *(Fig. 2, page 47)*,  working **around** sc row and in sc at base of sts on Row 2 *(Fig. A)*, skip next 2 sc, 7 dc in next sc, ★ skip next 2 sc, dc in next sc, skip next 2 sc, 7 dc in next sc; repeat from ★ across to last 3 sc, skip next 2 sc, (sc, ch 3, sc) in free loop of ch at base of last sc; working around dc at end of rows, skip first sc row, 5 dc in next row, (sc in next row, 5 dc in next row) across to last row, (sc, ch 3, sc) in last row; slip st in first dc of last row worked, leaving top edge unworked, finish off.

Fig. A

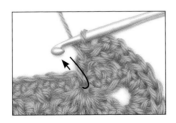

37

ON THE GO

■☐☐☐ **BEGINNER +**

SHOPPING LIST

Yarn (Medium Weight)
**[2.8 ounces, 162 yards
(80 grams, 148 meters) per skein]:**
☐ 10{13} skeins

Crochet Hook
☐ **Single Strand:** Size I (5.5 mm)
☐ **Double Strand:** Size M/N (9 mm)
or size needed for gauge

SIZE INFORMATION
Finished Size: 36" x 45"
(91.5 cm x 114.5 cm)

Size Note: We have printed the instructions for Single Strand and Double Strand versions in different colors to make it easier for you to find:
• Single Strand in Blue
• Double Strand (holding two strands of yarn together as one) in Pink
Instructions in Black apply to both versions.

Our photography model is a Single Strand blanket.

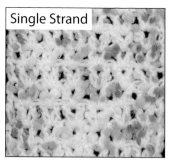

Single Strand

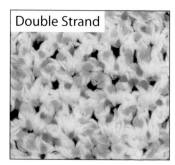

Double Strand

GAUGE INFORMATION

Single Strand, in pattern,
   14 dc = 4¹/₄" (10.75 cm),
   9 rows = 4" (10 cm)
Gauge Swatch: 4¹/₄"w x 4"h
   (10.75 cm x 10 cm)
Ch 16.
Work same as Body for 9 rows;
finish off: 6 2-dc groups and 2 dc.

Double Strand, in pattern,
10 dc = 4³/₄" (12 cm),
   6 rows = 4" (10 cm)
Gauge Swatch: 4³/₄"w x 4"h
   (12 cm x 10 cm)
Ch 12.
Work same as Body for 6 rows;
finish off: 4 2-dc groups and 2 dc.

INSTRUCTIONS
BODY

Ch 118{76}.

Row 1 (Wrong side)**:** 2 Dc in fourth ch from hook **(3 skipped chs count as first dc)**, place marker in same ch for Edging placement, (skip next ch, 2 dc in next ch) across to last 2 chs, skip next ch, dc in last ch: 57{36} 2-dc groups and 2 dc.

Note: Loop a short piece of yarn around the **back** of any stitch on Row 1 to mark **right** side.

Row 2: Ch 3 **(counts as first dc)**, turn; skip next dc, 📹 2 dc in sp **before** next dc (center of 2-dc group) *(Fig. 3, page 47)*, 2 dc in center sp of each 2-dc group across to last 2 dc, skip next dc, dc in last dc.

Repeat Row 2 for pattern until Body measures approximately 44¹/₄{44}"/112.5{112} cm from beginning ch, ending by working a **right** side row; do **not** finish off.

EDGING

Rnd 1: Ch 1, turn; 3 sc in first dc, sc in next dc and in each dc across to last 2 dc, skip next dc, 3 sc in last dc; 2 sc in end of each row across to last row, sc in last row;  working in free loops of beginning ch *(Fig. 2, page 47)*, 3 sc in first ch, sc in each ch across to marked ch, skip marked ch, 3 sc in next ch; 2 sc in end of each row across to last row, sc in last row; join with slip st to first sc.

Rnd 2: Ch 1, turn; ★ sc in next sc, ch 1, (skip next sc, sc in next sc, ch 1) across to next corner 3-sc group, skip next sc, (3 sc, ch 1) twice in center sc, skip next sc; repeat from ★ around; join with slip st to first sc, finish off.

PLAY MAT

■■□□ EASY

SHOPPING LIST

Yarn (Medium Weight)
[3.5 ounces, 207 yards
(100 grams, 188 meters) per skein]:
☐ 8{11} skeins

Crochet Hook
☐ Single Strand: Size I (5.5 mm)
☐ Double Strand: Size M/N (9 mm)
or size needed for gauge

SIZE INFORMATION
Finished Size: 37{37³/₄}" x 45"
[94{96} cm x 114.5 cm]

Size Note: We have printed the
instructions for Single Strand and
Double Strand versions in different
colors to make it easier for you to
find:
• Single Strand in Blue
• Double Strand (holding two strands
  of yarn together as one) in Pink
Instructions in Black apply to both
versions.

Our photography model
is a Single Strand blanket.

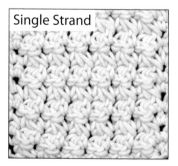
Single Strand

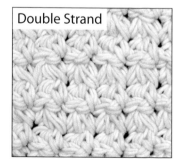
Double Strand

GAUGE INFORMATION

Single Strand, in pattern,
  7 repeats (14 sts) and 12 rows =
  4" (10 cm)
Gauge Swatch: 4" (10 cm) square
Ch 14.
Work same as blanket for 12 rows;
finish off: 14 sts.

Double Strand, in pattern,
  7 repeats (14 sts) and 10 rows =
  5¹/₂" (14 cm)
Gauge Swatch: 5¹/₂" (14 cm)
  square
Ch 14.
Work same as blanket for 10 rows;
finish off: 14 sts.

── STITCH GUIDE ──

📹 **BEGINNING CLUSTER**
  (uses next 3 chs)
★ Pull up a loop in same ch as last
st made and in next 2 chs, YO and
draw through all 4 loops on hook.
📹 **CLUSTER**
★ Working in chs and in sts, pull up
a loop in same st as last st made
and in next 2 sts, YO and draw
through all 4 loops on hook.

INSTRUCTIONS

Ch 130{96}.

Row 1: Sc in second ch from hook,
(work Beginning Cluster, ch 1)
across, sc in same ch as last st
made: 130{96} sts.

Row 2: Ch 1, turn; sc in first sc,
(work Cluster, ch 1) across to last sc,
sc in last sc.

Repeat Row 2 for pattern until
blanket measures approximately
45" (114.5 cm) from beginning ch.

Finish off.

general instructions

ABBREVIATIONS

ch	chain(s)
cm	centimeters
dc	double crochet(s)
hdc	half double crochet(s)
mm	millimeters
Rnd(s)	Round(s)
sc	single crochet(s)
sp(s)	space(s)
st(s)	stitch(es)
YO	yarn over

SYMBOLS & TERMS

★ — work instructions following ★ as many **more** times as indicated in addition to the first time.

† to † — work all instructions from first † to second † **as many** times as specified.

( ) or [ ] — work enclosed instructions **as many** times as specified by the number immediately following **or** work all enclosed instructions in the stitch or space indicated **or** contains explanatory remarks.

colon (:) — the number(s) given after a colon at the end of a row or round denote(s) the number of stitches or spaces you should have on that row or round.

GAUGE

Exact gauge is essential for proper size. Before beginning your blanket, make the sample swatch given in the individual instructions in the yarn and hook specified. After completing the swatch, measure it, counting your stitches and rows carefully. If your swatch is larger or smaller than specified, make another, changing hook size to get the correct gauge. **Keep trying until you find the size hook that will give you the specified gauge.**

MULTIPLES

When working Rnd 1 of some of the Edgings, it is necessary to work a multiple of 3 sc evenly across the side of the Body. Spacing the sc evenly so that the Body lays flat, work across to within 1" (2.5 cm) of the corner. Count your stitches in groups of 3, then work across the remaining side maintaining a multiple of 3 sc.

CROCHET TERMINOLOGY

UNITED STATES		INTERNATIONAL
slip stitch (slip st)	=	single crochet (sc)
single crochet (sc)	=	double crochet (dc)
half double crochet (hdc)	=	half treble crochet (htr)
double crochet (dc)	=	treble crochet(tr)
treble crochet (tr)	=	double treble crochet (dtr)
double treble crochet (dtr)	=	triple treble crochet (ttr)
triple treble crochet (tr tr)	=	quadruple treble crochet (qtr)
skip	=	miss

■□□□ BEGINNER	Projects for first-time crocheters using basic stitches. Minimal shaping.
■■□□ EASY	Projects using yarn with basic stitches, repetitive stitch patterns, simple color changes, and simple shaping and finishing.
■■■□ INTERMEDIATE	Projects using a variety of techniques, such as basic lace patterns or color patterns, mid-level shaping and finishing.
■■■■ EXPERIENCED	Projects with intricate stitch patterns, techniques and dimension, such as non-repeating patterns, multi-color techniques, fine threads, small hooks, detailed shaping and refined finishing.

Yarn Weight Symbol & Names	LACE 0	SUPER FINE 1	FINE 2	LIGHT 3	MEDIUM 4	BULKY 5	SUPER BULKY 6
Type of Yarns in Category	Fingering, 10-count crochet thread	Sock, Fingering Baby	Sport, Baby	DK, Light Worsted	Worsted, Afghan, Aran	Chunky, Craft, Rug	Bulky, Roving
Crochet Gauge* Ranges in Single Crochet to 4" (10 cm)	32-42 double crochets**	21-32 sts	16-20 sts	12-17 sts	11-14 sts	8-11 sts	5-9 sts
Advised Hook Size Range	Steel*** 6,7,8 Regular hook B-1	B-1 to E-4	E-4 to 7	7 to I-9	I-9 to K-10.5	K-10.5 to M-13	M-13 and larger

*GUIDELINES ONLY: The chart above reflects the most commonly used gauges and hook sizes for specific yarn categories.

** Lace weight yarns are usually crocheted on larger-size hooks to create lacy openwork patterns. Accordingly, a gauge range is difficult to determine. Always follow the gauge stated in your pattern.

*** Steel crochet hooks are sized differently from regular hooks—the higher the number the smaller the hook, which is the reverse of regular hook sizing.

CROCHET HOOKS																
U.S.	B-1	C-2	D-3	E-4	F-5	G-6	7	H-8	I-9	J-10	K-10½	L-11	M/N-13	N/P-15	P/Q	Q	S
Metric - mm	2.25	2.75	3.25	3.5	3.75	4	4.5	5	5.5	6	6.5	8	9	10	15	16	19

WORKING AROUND A STITCH

Work in stitch indicated, inserting hook in direction of arrow *(Fig. 1)*.

Fig. 1

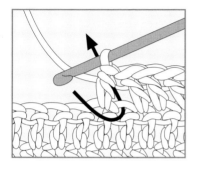

WORKING IN SPACE BEFORE A STITCH

When instructed to work in space **before** a stitch or in spaces **between** stitches, insert hook in space indicated by arrow *(Fig. 3)*.

Fig. 3

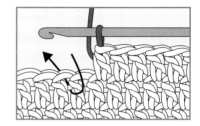

FREE LOOPS OF A CHAIN

When instructed to work in free loops of a chain, work in loop indicated by arrow *(Fig. 2)*.

Fig. 2

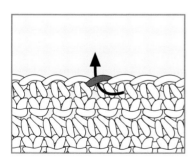

yarN iNForMaTioN

The blankets in this book were made using medium weight yarn. Any brand of medium weight yarn may be used. It is best to refer to the yardage/meters when determining how many skeins or balls to purchase. Remember, to arrive at the finished size, it is the GAUGE/TENSION that is important, not the brand of yarn.

For your convenience, listed below are the yarns used to create our photography models.

NAP TIME
Bernat® Li'l Tots™
#42730 Cool Blue

QUIET MOMENT
Red Heart® Super Saver®
#0381 Light Blue

SWEETIE PIE
Patons® Canadiana™
#10320 Cherished
   Lavender

ROCK-A-BYE
Red Heart®
   Soft Baby Steps®
#9702 Strawberry

PARTY TIME
Red Heart® Gumdrop™
#0501 Smoothie

STORY TIME
Red Heart®
   Soft Baby Steps™
#9620 Baby Green

SUNSHINE
Deborah Norville
Everyday®
   Soft Worsted
#1003 Baby Yellow

CLOUD SOFT
Red Heart® Soft® Yarn
#4600 White

CUDDLER
Lion Brand®
   Pound of Love®
#101 Pastel Pink

FUN TIME
Caron® Simply Soft®
#0015 Strawberry

ON THE GO
Bernat® Dippity Dots™
#66005 White

PLAY MAT
Lion Brand®
   Cotton-Ease®
#099 Almond

Production Team: Writer/Technical Editor - Cathy Hardy; Editorial Writer – Susan Frantz Wiles; Senior Graphic Artist – Lora Puls; Graphic Artist - Cailen Cochran; Photo Stylist - Sondra Daniel; and Photographer - Ken West.

Instructions tested and photo models made by Janet Akins, JoAnn Bowling, Marianna Crowder, Lee Ellis, Raymelle Greening, and Dale Potter.